On Holiday

John David Thompson

First Printing, First Edition

PALINDROME PUBLISHING OF IOWA
Pella, Iowa

Manufactured in the United States of America
Library of Congress Catalogue Number: 2007934409
ISBN: 9780972071758
Cover and layout design: Karisa Runkel

Palindrome Publishing of Iowa
Pella, IA

CONTACT POET AT
statepoetpro@yahoo.com

This book is dedicated

to

Marjorie Marie Hindes Thompson,

Christmas Baby, 1931

CONTENTS

CONTENTS

CONTENTS

CONTENTS

On Holiday

Cardinal Rules

The cardinal is the Christmas bird.

He takes birth-blood to wing—

To color a world on holiday—

Upon dusted boughs of evergreen.

The Arctic Hare

The arctic hare has speed
to spare—
quick not to muff
free foot.

For if his fur rolls slow,
it's *Ho! Ho! Ho!*—trapped
around Santa's trimmed hat
and suit.

Santa's Sestina

The house of Nestlenod is fast asleep.
No gross rodent moves, not even a nick.
The two children have waited for Christmas Eve,
both heads, bulbs of dreams. Arrival is as
planned: Santa Claus pipes down the chimney. Cold
from the world, he bobbles to the tree skirt.

He lays the normal gifts first: sock, gloves, skirt—
typical fare, not a fantastic leap
from last year's gear. Good! The milk is not cold,
but the cookies, *ugh*, and who took a nick
out of each one? Not a single crumb will pass
his palate, though a few catch his fur sleeve.

A check of his list, yep, these kids believe.
The jolly elf rewards them with a kiss-curt
message, *Thanks for the treats, and, yes, the glass*
of warm milk. Atop the roof, one deer leaps
before looking, as antlers and hoof nick
a northside bush, and freeze like they're pickled.

Claus takes a big-belly pause—the house, old
friend. The master, once, a child here, retriev-
ing presents of the past, left by St. Nick—
before electronic game wars that hurt
what's left of handmade nostalgia. The sleet
on the pane scurries him to finish—*fas*....

Santa's Sestina

Dasher...Dancer...Give it some glacial gas!
He summons the team. In his teeth, Blitz holds
black reins. It's slick, this roof, one faith, one leap—
against the moon, a silhouette, an eve—
ning comet darkens the sky. The sleigh skirts
to next village. The job is no picnic.

Morning is the first gift from ol' St. Nich—
olas. The Nestlenods waken and pass
each downward stair in hopes the tree inert
with unwrappables and dreams to unfold.
Honest all the down hours, not a one eaves—
dropping on North Pole knocking during small sleep.

Upon the tree's skirt, a doll who loves in her sleep,
best truck, folk knick-knacks, and a babe suckled
by the breaths each Eve, the night before—*Twas*.

Airing Christmas Laundry

The myth will rinse; when it cleans, the lint knows
Old stories from Santa won't wash the air
And, still, kids cling, stubborn as static snow

Parents basket the blunders, quick to tow
The wet disappointment, the bleaching stares
The myth will rinse; when it cleans, the lint knows

Hampered by betrayal, children red-glow
A sort-and-separate eye to fading fare
And, still, kids cling, stubborn as static snow

Hung-out-to dry from the cold water soak
A fluff, a fold—cycle leaves children bare
The myth will rinse; when it cleans, the lint knows

Folks forgiven for dirty linen, though
Some stains remain, tumbling, to stiff despair
And, still, kids cling, stubborn as static snow

We begin our spin—kids believe the load
Left on the line pinned with fine lies to spare
The myth will rinse; when it cleans, the lint knows
And, still, kids cling, stubborn as static snow

First Christmas Lullaby

A child's first Christmas is a swaddle of baby blue
The sky and beasts are calm; Santa is unpacking soon
A child's first Christmas is swaddle of baby blue
To warm tufts of manger hair

A child's first Christmas, a bundle to waltz downtown
The folks of Christmases past gather around
A child's first Christmas, a bundle to waltz downtown
To shine with silver songs peeling in crisp air

A child's first Christmas is a binding bow
One holiday down, the miles of more ties to go
A child's first Christmas is a binding bow
The gift received goes on

A child's first Christmas is an anxious eye
Though he may not speak, the infant is wise
A child's first Christmas is an anxious eye
Come snow, come sleigh, come son

Sleep well, fresh boy, beneath reaching star
We share blankets of snow and sand—how they stretch far—
Just like our prayers, our boundless hearts—

Signed,
The Kids Who Live Downstairs

The Combs and the Fob

After THE GIFT OF THE MAGI

Her hair is gone.
It might as well be her heart.
Nothing so beautiful ever graced the flat.
And so it is.
It is just as well.
But our tortoise teeth cannot return to the shell.

His watch is gone.
It might as well be his mind.
No time so logical ever paced the flat.
And so it is.
Alas, brush-jewels, do not resign.
My platinum strap is fussy; here, comb mine.

Matchless

After Hans Christian Andersen's THE LITTLE MATCH GIRL

What light, what heat
sticks like friction
in hungry hair—
no match for Despair.

Old Amsterdam—

I stand before the hoary corpse
of the Little Match Girl,
hung holly, sad sulfur.

Breaths of despair,
my boots attend
in storybook wonder.

If only I had purchased
a fascicle of her wares,
No.

If only I had been sufficient wind
to avert strike, her father's fury,
No.

If only I were the fire
she could not
put out.

Wait a Last Minute, Shopper

You've paid for your last-minute bundle.
You've passed the twelve-items-or-fewer clerk.
Twelve minutes last until the twelve days of Christmas.
Come, look inside Salvation's wrapped box.
Oh, scurrier, what could it hurt?
You peer into a dark theatre, nearly.
You see perhaps a doll and a tin.
Your stocking-bound lipstick falls from your bustling bags.
You can't have that! Go on. Retrieve it. Reach in.

Mercy. Can you put a finger on it?

Threads of Pitiful Pearl depreciate your gilded finger.
Discount's drum makes a stick of your thumb.
A special blue light sheds roofless joy on Army's barn,
almost barren.
You wonder as red gloss wanders your roam-hand. How come?
What makes that tight skin beat?
What makes that poor stitch smile?
Of all toys galore in picked-over store,
they, for certain, tonight, will be with a child.

And So This Is Salvation

Five minutes to six—The retail doors about to close.
You've got yo-yo's, gum sticks, play putty
at the counter, things you chose to close up
Christmas shopping –then off like a stream pennant
you and your fur wrap go, Christmas, go!

But as you and the PETA protested
trot past the last revolving glass,
leaving behind thumbed-over toys,
toys that must wait—at least—one Christmas more,
your own lipstick falls in a box of Salvation Army allure.

You peer into the abyss of near abandon, near dark,
then fondle a plush penguin, a case of colored chalk,
until you grab the gloss for which you fought
lip-and-tooth for a few hours back
at the High Echelon Salon and Cosmetics Shop.

You lift the make-up as aisle speakers wail of the mild and meek.
then blindly, you rouge nobody's doll, nobody's child, wet in her sleep—
the flavor of Cherry's Charity streams like penance down her cheek.

Poor, Pitiful Pearl

Named for a concealed gem,
hardened by depressed times,
in the assembly-line ocean,
she is hooked and lured
by icons of Poverty and Concern
to live the rest of her days
as a peculiar doll on earth.

An anachronism to those
who have gone toy-fishing,
her tawdry hair, irregular face,
more fit for Great Decline of the 30s.
Poor Pitiful Pearl is out of place
in the aisle and age of first Barbies,
even within the discount bin—ordinary disgrace.

And on her sullied hem,
a scarlet patch, not unlike Hester Prynne,
who can match Pearl's disbelief to the letter;
for it is not little girls, little girls, who buy
this should-be-retail-reject
too impoverished to wear a disguise—
not little girls, but grown women
who through their 50s furs, fat purses remember—

When nothing in the kitchen stewed,
FDR announced entry in World War II,
and not even a whiskered tree or stocking stirred
in their pale houses of bleakest Decembers.

--for Little Marjorie

(All I Want for Christmas Is) A Macy's Thanksgiving Float

All I want for Christmas is a Macy's Thanksgiving float.
Think about it.
After the parade brisks by,
Where are those heavenly-heliums to go?
I've got a float-flat waiting for Flying Ace Snoopy
In my Upper West Manhattan backyard.
No, I am not blowing hot air.
Don't rain on my tirade!
I really want one!
A regal tree-topper fresh from barking Central Park,
To be my neighborhood watchdog,
Not a stuffed-plush stacked among a hundred
In a beagle pyramid at Macy's Department Store.
A crime is committed in New York every 8 seconds.
I need all the height and hound I can muster.
I'll be standing at Columbus Circle.
Lift the sandbags! Doff the nets!
Santa, be a good Rockefeller.
Bring a bereft balloon to me.
(All's fair after Time's Square.)
Give the holiday deflated some afterlife cheer.

—for Clay

Snow Angels

wwwwww

Children of divorce, December's dust,
Left behind the blade,
Messengers of the fell run, collision course—
Both Dad's 'kerchief and Ma's cap have made.

They are the paper dolls
Santa forgot to deliver.
See them lying in winter waves—
Fleeced, worried wings—
Haling down his sleigh—
As he leaves each Eve—
Banked and born, perfectly torn—
To wrestle the weight of Earth's negligent shiver.

Luminous

Your youngest looks through the new Christmas cards
and reads the word *luminous*.

What does loominus mean?
He asks.

Maybe you'll get a dictionary from Santa and find out.
You reply.

That night, he opens the first gift.
Doesn't matter among the clatter
What it is—
A light from the tree angel
Strings his eye.
His heart, like a harp, sings.

And it's Mom who finds out what *luminous* means.

Bedford Falls

George Bailey is discouraged.
Money is missing from his building and loan,
So is his faith.

The town of Bedford Falls is a patchwork choir
Of Christmas Eve prayer—
Gowan's Drugstore, Martini's, the Garage, sweet wife Mary.

But Hee-Haw George is too miserable
Doing slippery bridgework
To notice the quiet urgencies beneath worried roofs.

The town would not be the same
Without him.
That is the Capraesque truth.

Enter Clarence, with a rabbit's IQ,
Hopping hard-luck George place-to-place
Around Potter's would-be village of debauchery, disgrace.

Why if Peyton needed
A home
Potter's would be the Place.

The necessity of one—
George wakes and runs through a fast snow.
What Clarence-clarity it brings.

A bell welcomes two babes,
The Birth of Our Lord, Jesus Christ,
And an angel earning first-class wings.

--for Kent Fetty

Christmas Carpenters

Jesus was a carpenter,
so he joined the alto of an angel
with the composure of a pop-maestro
to create Karen and Richard Carpenter.

The best carpenter tool, it is said,
is one that requires the least effort
upon its user—the listener—
smooth, ear candy.

No one covered Nat Kings Cole's
Chestnuts like Karen's version.
No one dare to cover the Carpenters'
Merry Christmas, Darling.

Sound renowned,
some sirens try to copy, though,
their elfish efforts pale
like bleached mistletoe.

Stevie Nicks and Old St. Nick

Rumour has it,
'Twas the Christmas Eve of Tambourines,
stockings hung pinned to gypsy shawls,
paper flowers of white wing
in fireplace singed,
upstairs slept rock-and-roll's porcelain doll.

When amidst her gold-dust dreams,
there came such a landslide lean,
an enchanted entrance by one so jolly,
that she rose to the edge—
of seventeen-foot bed
and poured herself an I-can't-wait hot toddy.

Who's there? Talk to me, the sorcerer spoke
from her crystal lair;
when no one answered,
this her decision:
to descend the dreams-unwind
Shangri-la stair,
and this her stand-back vision:

St. Nick in fresh soot and platform boots
of leather and lace;
the rest in a belch of fur.
He took Sara's hand—
She said, *Wait a minute, baby.*
Man! Was he about to welsh her?

Stevie Nicks and Old St. Nick

Stevie Nicks and Old St. Nick

It came upon a mirage clear,
star above the chandelier,
all planets and universe forgot.
Santa and Stevie, like ghosts of past Christmas Evies,
soared above clouds of audience roar
to a mid 1970s parking lot
where Lindsey Buckingham delivered Miss Nicks
some very bad second-hand news.
A signature song was to be dismissed, cut.

Good Claus did bring
through his beard of silver springs,
a message: *Stevie, in time, you'll outlive him.*
His gift like a bell that night, rang with advice:
Love of his life, forgive him.

The Snow Fox

A college junior completes the last question on the Miller Analogies Test:

TRICK : FOOL :: (A. blizzard B. fox C. hail D. flummox) : SNOW

A. blizzard--she ovals.

TRICK IS TO FOOL AS BLIZZARD IS TO SNOW.

B. FOX-THE ANSWER GIVEN IN THE BACK—

WITH EXPLANATION.

TO TRICK IS TO FOOL, WHEREAS TO FOX IS TO SNOW.

The snow fox knows
when and where
to bare the blind stare
of his arctic coat—

after the last trick
has been bagged
like a candied leaf
in late October;

but before the first
fool salivates to the trill
of the japer's two-tapered hat
in nascent April.

The Road Winter

The crest of solstice,
fallen cusp of day—Two horses—
octet fetlocks, in equine motion
yoking a cherry sleigh

He in brownstone bonnet
She in fedora fur hat
A fistful of frost at the rein
Muffled thought on her lap

Solitaire's spruce, ladies-of-red-sage
Along, ablaze, old road less graveled—
Like a Christmas carillon, countryside,
The pave, a dowdy white swan in her seventh age

A garland of skins, mutual thought—candle and inn
Run as a team, press both passengers forward
Each mile a gust, veer, yaw, and thrust
Dust-bare, snow-boned—*Onward, You Sorrels!*

Mare and masterpiece, hide by hide
Hoof and horse, dame and Sir Deed
(Recall, good reader, this scurry
A mid-19th century ride)

Framed trail receives brush with nostalgia
Like Torme's roasting-to-be of chestnut fires
This lithograph, an autograph

Signed,

Currier and Ives

Nivea Campana

Henry Wadsworth Longfellow wrote the poem "Christmas Bells"
later to be the lyric "I Heard the Bells on Christmas Day," Christmas Day, 1863,
while nursing his son Charles, wounded in the Civil War.

He had an ear for war, that Longfellow,
knowing no two forms were ever alike—

Holocaust home for the holidays,
cannon flickering o'er candle-kegged windows,

a peal of sable-scarved cardinal
bloodying the yuletide sky.

Gave him the quills. Broke serenade into accursed song.

He had a belfry for lyric, that Longfellow,
a wounded son and nation remembered on every line—

Hollow Christmas Eve, 1863,
Gettysburg and son Charles in a sling—doleful snow, doleful snow.

Pale epitaphs bunched, forted,
building old, familiar dirges on high.

Kept the man at home, away from the caroling throng.

He had an ear for silver, that Longfellow,
the kind that flanked Christendom, then rang from the chest,

Holy Ghosts scrooging around elsewhere in England,
what rightful apparition could redress this civil wrong?

Predatory bells tolled the passing,
bleak season drifted on hungry tongues.

The first chime was *ding* The dead ringer was *dong*.

Silver Tells

Speak, December, Speak!
Tongues of silver seize the streets.
Bells chime winter's clime.

Achoo Haiku

Winter tips its blade
Icicle-inked judges rate
Flakes of figure eight

A Fleming Carol

Nullaig Shona Duit-the Irish Merry Christmas—
pronounced null-ig hun-a dit—means
to one and all.

Good Irish all—at yule time
Shannon draws her shawl of river rime
To bear the beast of winter clime
Now, neighbor, whitewash yours
And I will lime rinse mine
Nollaig Shona Duit
All raise a Dublin pint of emerald shine

The Brownes, The Codds
The Lymans, the Hayes
The Walshes, the McMurroughs
Inhabit the kin-warmth of basin-place
A sacred candle
Windows each holy house and face
Such is the beauty
Of ancient grace

As for me, this seanchai lass has ne'er crossed
The Wexford County line
Though my paddy is an Ulster brine
Me heart with his, and his to mine
Nollaig Shona Duit
The holly of Leinster longs to leave
And twine with Londonderry's ivy vine

The turtle dove tails as two
The wrenboy drums, *Curoo, Curoo*
I weep at the breaking wave of isle news
Me Ulster brine laces his buskins
To battle alongside the might of Brian Boru

The Gaelic snow seasons the famined glen
Our village sustains without the hunt
Of our bounty men
For our ancestors gave to Her, what the past bade to Him
Lasses, be each your strength, the strength of ten

A Fleming Carol

A Fleming Carol

The land is low—spirits glass-eye high
The homebound folk seed the bread caraway
For eve is nigh
Each kitling and bantling becomes a spy
At cockcrow, *Arrah!*
In the midst of war
Father Christmas has not sluiced them by
Sir Yeats portends
On life, on death—cast a cold eye

A holiday of bloodguilt red
Seeps toward the green
The Lakes of Killarney jig and reel
Giggling like a limerick stream
I bless the farthest shore
And see me Brine above
The warring ships of Irish seas
Nollaig Shona Duit
Love, 'tis yours to dream

Elveswhere

The elves don't dance
in me wintering dreams.
Their agile agendas
simply *tee-hee-hee* refuse.

Sprig-like sprites
won't light one ignite
in me reverie hair—
What's a yuletide yawner to do?

I've a nary a fairy
up me slumbering sleeve—
'Tis true
'Tis blue.

I wake to slip on
me sorry soles—
Oops!
Two are in me shoes!

Have a Santa and a Smile

He is the real thing,
even cola rivals colactively agree.
Haddon Sundblom's rendition
of the intruder-at-holiday tradition
is a hoof-leap and roof-bound
beyond the rest, the one you want
delivering your wish list each Christmas Eve.

This is the human Santa,
with a believable face,
a cotton patch for a beard
brown boots too busty for laces.

He's timely and tender.
Why not? He drinks
the world's refresher
about his global rounds.

And don't children peering
behind an old chair
look cuter, more innocent,
when sizing the man
who just came to town?

Of Fizzer, On Sipper
On Capper, On Sale!

You can hear him cry out
behind moustache of angel-hair bale.

On Guzzler! On Quencher!
On Pauser! On Ice!

To all a nostalgic season!
And to thirst, a good night!

Christmas Narcissus

Narcissus papyraceus

Pine of December, and I'm up again.
Look at me! Still being—white ribbons, bows.
Show me a gauzed mirror; I'll show you self's friend—
Full of flawless gifts, interior snows.

You know the poinsettia, you know the rose.

So.

I climb my own ringed stalk, reach Christmas Eve,
Bear my groomed beans, beauties in white.
Mistletoe below, envy my pearl sleeves.
'Tis not pleasure in rising, but diaphanous delight.

I look true East, these kings will lay down
What they can for low-cradled—dirt, myrrh, sand;
I'm sure I've a tear-pool, room for three crowns.
Desert lords leave for me, a reverence grand.

Epiphany's bride! echo all papers.

No.

By botany, I'll never be flower girl for a savior.

American Duty

She is always
under the roses
beneath the bed
where earth's
bed is wine.
What is here--
horizons deny me,
vertigo abides me,
the axis scents
of sex & sky.
This grasp for lattice
on behalf of lover,
between chaste lacework,
thorns of twenty,
Descent, I climb;
for she is always
under the roses.
Pause—but
do not bring her.
Inhale hereafter.
(possess time)

Appointment with Poinsettia

Hola!
Come closer, child.
I promise I won't bite.
My, but it's poignant tonight.
Sit here,
in the Enlightenment Chair.
Let's see. You want just the bracts.
Where to begin? Oh, yes… *'Twas the night.*

You look old enough to me, kick,
to have heard a myth or two.
That's it. Stroke my scarlet leaves.
I've something to dispel to you.

Those of us who bring beauty,
euphoric pulchritude,
to the season, those of us
donning blessed red—
odd Rudolph,
a blush in Bethlehem,
even I—we've had to bear rumor,
great falsehoods,
a thorn of prejudgments
gaveled into our noses, crib, and whorling heads.

A light through foggy night,
suckling Savior for humankind's sin,
a captured wild Mexican rose—
annual ambassadors to this world of woe—
yes, those shunned at games,
nailed in wrath's flames,
seeds spread with Tannenbaum talk,

Taste the flower's milk, kid; and it's to the doctor
or deathbed you go.

Appointment with Poinsettia

Appointment with Poinsettia

This Christmas Eve—
You call it, kid—
sweet of indulgence,
toy of electronic spoils,
limbs of artifice in lieu of fresh tree.

Go ahead.
Name your poison.

But don't you dare, love,
name me.

The Town Square

APOTHECARY
drug store
WALMART

COBBLERY
shoe store
WALMART

WEB

STATIONERY
gift shop
WALMART

CONFECTIONERY
sweet shop
WALMART

Loving Someone Jewish

He tells you Hannukah is older than Christmas,
And, if you have, an hour, he will light
Your Christian mind about the lives of the Jews.
The Second World War was but in a long procession of oppression.
The lighted hour of your enlightenment ignites into two.
He speaks of rededication, the rightful surge of the Maccabees,
A Temple for cleansing—
The hour spins like a Dreidel to three.
He touches your cold skin with warm oil—
And reinforces its importance for candle's burn and potato's bake.
The time has flown like Divine Diaspora.
You mind is lit like a menorah, a single hour,
Spreads to miraculous eight.

The life of Christ has not come between you.
No fires of denial fell from the evergreen.
Not an angel interrupted by saying,
Forget the Jew and follow me.
You are in love with someone Jewish.
He's in love with someone of Christian cause.

Eight tiny lights lift you through his winter celebration of struggle.
Eight tiny reindeer lift him through incredulity of Santa Claus.

--for BA

Snowfall, Downtown Des Moines

The scene is why a lyricist paved
city sidewalks, busy sidewalks
several silver-bell tolls ago.

It is a light, but most influential snow,
a swarm-of-scurry, guide of cold-blooded ghosts,
prompting a silver-belled shopper on Locust Street where to go.

The insurance buildings, like bold toy soldiers,
stand guard in gray over her—
list, parasol, and purse.

Like overflow mistletoe, a speaker hangs
from dandruffed utility pole. Caroler Karen Carpenter
sings a home-for-the-holidays verse.

The Christmas lights, this year, are neon holly,
a funeral of fern procession,
proportional, one wreath, alternates, per half-block.

Down here, downtown—
The Equitable Building is her Father Christmas,
its beard trimmed with red brick and granite from Vermont.

The dressing snow drifts from boot lash to memory,
as nothing but the woman's self-reflection stands
a manikin as if inside an empty Younker's store window.

The aged lady extends a last-minute hand,
cold brush of glass reminds her—
It's not the most wonderful time of the year, for a widow.

Terrace Hill at Christmastime

The Hubbell family is often considered,
The First Family of Des Moines, Iowa.
Frederick Cooper Hubbell married Mary Windsor, December 26, 1889.
However, it was sister Beulah Cooper Hubbell's marriage to the Count of Sweden
at Terrace Hill Mansion, May 2, 1899, that was billed
Iowa's social event of the century.
The poem is an English sonnet in honor of the Victorian, high day of the Hubbells.

Autumn has served its term at Terrace Hill.
Grounds men tuck Indian summer away.
Winter-elect steps to the lectern sill.
Time for yule season to inaugurate.

When through black walnut doors of the estate,
a bride and groom in Victorian garb,
bolt down Grand Avenue in Hubbell sleigh,
past blue spruce lifting stunned boughs in the yard.

Oh, it's Mary and Fred's annual ride—
the two turtledoves wed the day after Christmas morn—
He is tuxed to the 1889s.
She, brocaded in beige satin galore.

One hundred years, couple waited, you see—
Beulah's *I do* to Count booked last century.

The Skate at Scholte Gardens

Part I: A Pella, Iowa, Christmas Trilogy

As the good folks of Pella
simmer down, in mid-December,
for a gentle, concord snow—
the bronze statues at Scholte Gardens
rise to life from iron, despite the tin of record lows.

The gardener boards his bike
to enter the wintry gate
and wonder of chilled flowers.
Grown lady and daughter stowed
behind her quite copper dress,
reborn as human forms,
though keep it quiet,
for it is after-hours.

And the two cast tulips
a boy of brass offers in blooming hands,
they change into a pair of wooden skates.
He slips them on like woolen stockings,
glides about the iced brick lawn—
but not in the usual figure 8s.

As *S* for snow,
An *S* for Savior,
Then Boy Brinker judges himself a pause—
to catch fresh breath
for the biggest *S* yet—
one for Sinterklass.

Gardener, Woman, and Daughter
gather around such Dutch performance of astound—
a gesture of gratitude to deliver—
there—at the boy's momentary, flesh feet
a fallen treat—
tulips of bell and silver.

The Dutch Letters of Your Mind

Part II: A Pella, Iowa, Christmas Trilogy

Like a curve upon a curve
Where convex and concave meet
Holy Holland to America's Amsterdam
The perfectionary pride of Franklin Street

Savor sugar, savor spice
Neither pinch nor few grains to waste
Chill, shape, and bake until Klokkenspel chimes
Tender flakes rise gingerly to house the almond paste

Mother and daughter greet scrumptious six at Jaarsma's
Blacksmith forges one-half dozen from Vander Ploeg's
Kin Folks from Attica and Knoxville speed their wheels
To grab checkered sacks to go

Like a sweet snail stationary
A tempting, slender slither into the City of Refuge
Thanks, Sinterklaas, may we have another?
Anxious clicks of wooden shoes

Dominie and Mareah Scholte founded this village
Surely, on the capital *S*
Nether children learn the 19th letter
Before reciting remains of the garden's alphabet

Trumpets to tulips! Word to your windmill—more smashing than
Pella Windows—Wyatt Earp, street scrubbers aside,
Nothing lingers on frontal-lobe fingers like these souvenirs
The Dutch letters of your mind

Sinterklaas

Part III: A Pella, Iowa, Christmas Trilogy

December 5th,
The Eve of St. Nicholas' Feast Day in The Netherlands

Anna places her woods earthed with carrots;
Jan slides his Klompen billowed with hay
beneath blue fires of early December
in Holland-hope Sinterklaas will descend Dutch way.

His white horse, Amerigo, will be hungry.
The fantastic sail from Spain
will have famished the sugar cubes from beard and beast
until miter and mount replenished again.

But what to leave Zwarte Piet?
Black Peter in outlander terms—
his face charred in soot from chimney dives,
or is Nick's surprise-assistant a racial slur?

The year's chosen harbor opens its arms for festive entry.
Questions sleep with carrots and hay another century.

Iceberg Rose, Greenwood Rose Garden, Des Moines

There, among an ocean of Bride's Dreams,
Tahitian Sunsets, and Starry Nights,
You spot the dispassionate beauty—
And your frigate for romance come-hithers
Toward her frigid fragrance.

Flirtatious tip, she reveals, at best,
Ten percent of total floral cluster—
But that is enough glacial-gather
To trip your maiden voyage,
Freeze you in your dinner jacket.

Starboard, the prow of your nose brushes her side—
Aromatic collide, flower to your fancy,
Lady breaks a bit—
Just enough to tear olfactory senses of all passengers—
Appreciation, up-turned in First Class—
                                                            curiosity in lower ranks.
Her battering bouquet sinks into your hull of memory.

Witness clouds are lifeboats   ported in an odorless sound.
Cold April, like first temptation,
Comes late this season, and so you inhale, and so you drown.

Captain, captive,
Your breath will never reach penance
At far side
Of garden-harbor.

Nearer to God, nearer to God—
You cry for a smell,
But it is she of spring's sea
Who is resistant to water
And men.
Her white habit could save souls—
Or devour them.

Albino Deer, St. Ansgar, Iowa

The Dickens of the Forest,
she may have seen three ghosts
morning of her spring birth—
they who scared, whitened, and seized
the color of her frame.

For eight years,
the chalk fawn removed paint
from dark timber lines between Minnesota, Iowa—
she who saw *red* at humankind's careless artistry—
keeping notes on her skin, the tint of fresh paint.

Fifteen upstart tails
would call the doe *mother* ,
though none of them, none of them
to take her pallor shade.

Nearly invisible all of her life,
our deer could not quite disappear,
like that one cloud of wonder
on an, otherwise, blue day.

But those ghosts reappeared,
like the slip of glass in winter,
trio of haunts—
pneumonia, kidney failure, and old age.

December 28, 1846

Winter stars are first candles we see.
We guest homesteaders—
We children of the Territory.
Christmas, as our families attend it—
Three eves past.
We've boxing to do—colors and wraps.
Our men are in Mexico, guiding a war.
We've snow up to our souls;
And the knee shakes of more.
The year is about to take to sleigh,
Bids sleepy plows beneath—warm, idle night.
The meadowlands, a white card;
We pioneer forms have our histories to inscribe:

Between observed birth of Our Savior
And fresh calendar's first day,
Iowa pushes the coldest of irons to become a state—
While the rest of the nation is on holiday.

Wine Speakeasy

Softly, wine has been a part
of Christmas seasons, softly,
like a learned ghost trying
to teach an old friend
a memorable lesson on giving.

Wine knew the Monks
who raised primitive mugs
hundreds of years
before the birth of Christ
and saw an oracle.

And it is a soft line between
drunk/and merry.
Grapes don't wear well
in winter, though the vine
is suitable for the ice's clime.

Step with me softly, friend,
into the pantry this Christmas Eve.
Our lips receive fresh paint—red and lush.
Barefooted, we tipsy to the tree—
Confuse gifts for grapes—*Crush!*

Christmas Dream

I encounter it, annually,
in my willow sleep.
The Christmas dream rises
and bends through the mists
of rapid-eye movements
like a hothouse poinsettia
in its seasonal steam.

I am a package in Santa's bag,
bound to be tossed down a chimney
of soot and slag.
What is the point of dressing
me prim in a fattened box—
when I need to be dirty and slim
like a brief thief
to enter a house, residency, or resort?

The stiff sweater inside me itches;
I know whoever's kid will be disappointed.

It's crowded company here—
So why didn't the elves, in rehearsal,
show our holdings how to be
double-jointed?

Christmas Scar

A triolet sonnet

I call it my Christmas scar, unusual wound.
I earned the scarlet skate from a grate; I was two.
My brother and sisters shoved me up a heat-duct flue.
I call it my Christmas scar, unusual wound.
They told me, *Find out what Santa left us anew,*
as all pushed my tush from basement to first-floor view.
I call it my Christmas scar, unusual wound.
I earned the scarlet skate from a grate; I was two.

Did I say I was two? Well, perhaps I was three.
And maybe, just maybe, I had some smarts on me.
See, I made up lies about the upstairs inventory.
I told brother of a gun, both sisters of just-right bikes—
and dream houses, some shot shells, tassles –and the likes.
Oh, how they cried when truth unwrapped itself at first light.

Strike a Red Nose

DAZE	HAZE
OBSCURITY	ABSURDITY
MIST	WISP
PLACE	REINDEER

<u>**HERE**</u>

II
On Nativity

Evergreen at Christmastime

Love speaks a hush
o'er the nativity scene.
Love bows the shepherd's head
and the boughs of the evergreen.
A miracle in a manger—
World, have you a minute or two
to consider the gift God has given to you?

As a virgin rose
to greet the child in her calm hands,
peace was named his brother
throughout the orphaned land.
Love is room at the inn.
Enter in.
That is what humans long to do.

You and I
know the tree
by its lights
and the wings on high.
We care
for the children
beneath its
bows and bosom.

But do we
know eternal sky
by the sound of the boy's cry—
And do we care
in our duty and despair
if we ever hear him?

Evergreen at Christmastime

Evergreen at Christmastime

When the lights
are marred
by perennial push
and secular shove,
and our cares refuse
to fall as crumbs
at the fresh feet
of His glorious son.

Time has denied
neither the pine before the fire,
nor the pine
of the lamb's desire.
Come, winter,
with your quick thief of ice,
for nothing can splinter
our enduring in Jesus Christ.

This night,
lowers with birth
of morning weather,
beasts and a boy
among hay and treasures,
the first angel
atop spreading measures
of evergreen.

Christmas in the Wildwood

Little Brown Church in the Vale, Nashua, Iowa

He spoke to her on Christmas Eve,
Dear Amelia, don your wedding gown.
We've a destine to travel for your best present;
then, the spirited doves drove out of Waterloo, north of town.

The couple came to clearing
among fog wood in wintry down,
a familiar place of promise, old lace,
pledged by the betrothed in a sanctuary wrapped in brown.

Wife and husband returned to where it all began,
though a holly of welcome now hung on the door,
spread of poinsettia backlit the pastor and organ,
a drift of manger hay draped the church floor.

Inside a prayer lifted the veil to clarity; the witness snow did sift.
A knowing from newlyweds back to nativity: Love is the greatest gift.

Christmas at the Grotto

West Bend, Iowa

The question on every parishioner's mind
the first season holiday lights are to drape
the walls that drape the stations to the tomb:
Perhaps such bulbs, too far a break from reason, tradition—

Would Father Dobberstein approve?

My, the lavender twinkles suggest Brazilian amethyst;
the piercing white, Carrara stone.
The way some luminaries dip beneath
snowbound surface—it looks like angels
sojourning December's bend with heaven's glow.

But the hymn-holders at Saints Peter and Paul's Church unsettled
as volunteers check tentative strings for proper blinking.
Then, a cherub walks in, his eyes sing with a grin—

Look! It's Father Dobberstein winking!

Accessory to Divine

A gentleman wind strings the town with snow.
Streetlights bend their necks to accept the gift
Of weightless beads against dark velvet lift.
Night is an evening dress laced in white-buttoned glow.

We look at this courtship from misted panes
Like curious candles, eavesdropping elves
Who agree the town needs a night out on itself.
The blizzard's a beau; a cold, trusted flame.

A virgin white nests the morning to birth.
The good town is back home at reasonable hour.
She is all tongues; our ears brace for verbiage shower.
She speaks of a miracle beyond worth.

We disbelieve first, then faith's freeze clasps us.
He was born beneath such pearls of dust.

Christmas Bonus

Two last-hour shoppers
fumble for spilled change;
their destitute eyes
meet soon.

Each one, poorer, flips to the other;
What is lost to me is lost to you.

Consoling shoulders,
these Christmas Eve strangers
repaid in gold draws
of distant manger tune.

Each one, richer, coins to his brother.
What is born onto me is born onto you.

The Hierarchy of Angels

The Devil is general; angels are specific.

God being universal
Delegates discrete authority,
Establishes functional hierarchy
Among strata of angels

The Trinity, obsessed with Triumvirates
Spawns Three Orders:

Bearers of God's Throne,
Priests,
then Ministers

Each order wings Three Classes:

Bearers

Gabriel, the brass go-between & Cherubim, highest beneath God
Dancers of the intellect for the Omniscient Mind

The Seraphim
Breathing heaven's fire, the eternal, not infernal kind

The Thrones
Minders of the quake, unshaken by the raptures of being

The Hierarchy of Angels

The Hierarchy of Angels

Priests

The Lords
Who teach nations to govern without the dusting of towers

The Powers
Mighty mentors to soldiers of earth's inevitable dirt, battles

The Rulers
Keepers of spiritual truths & treasures, God's trove of priceless chattel

Ministers

The Principalities
Weathered ones of our upper ether

Archangels
Blessing the down, four-limbed, beastly creatures—
humankind's ablest teachers

At last, Angels
Lowly angels, bone-specific, still we laud them on high
Each a god on cross guard
Until we are permitted to walk the street lanes of the sky

The One Belief

Do you tell his smile at six,
or wait 'til he's elegant eight?
That it's Mom and Dad
who purchase the gifts
and lease treats out on a plate.

And will that pout take it all
in a snowball's stride—
be a seasonal sport—
when your boy realizes
his dreams have been untied
only to be clipped short?

Yes, it's enough
to cause any soccer Mom
to kick herself in her own net
when kids face the fibs:
there was never a list.

From those innocent chins—
parents witness
the abstract facts—
a look of wintry betrayal,
before thawing acceptance
frames reality's picture.

This, folks, is when you hold fast
to the remaining reins
and pull out the goodies of Gospel
sprinkled with Scripture.

Gertrude and Alma, Winter Spirits

Gertrude Hindes and Alma Thompson,
both deceased, are the poet's grandmothers
who lived in his hometown, Lamoni, Iowa.

The settled women in town
gather and wash garments
between funerals.

They have scaled seasons,
scrubbed mountainous walls,
in the same rooms

where
wounded dresses
were mended.

My own grandmothers are here,
sending last Christmas seals,
and it's time to go.

I know
by their eyes of Decembering rain
and hair of snow.

Pity the grandchild,
who knew all the words, but to say,
goodbye and thank you a might better—

as fresh winter spirits lift
into the highest
of weather.

Log on a Fire

Sacrifice has a place.
It breathes with hearth.
Winter wood beneath spits
of immaculate stars,
skewers the seasonal shish-ka-bob.
December partridges, blizzard lovebirds,
greet and coo a toast.
A marshmallow tans as it fattens.
The blackened chestnuts roast.
Wrapped in swaddling flames—
this log on a fire—
dying on a carpenter's cross of consuming desire.

Snowflakes of Bethlehem, I

Both snowflakes of Bethlehem
drift to the manger,

birth upon birth,
light upon light.

Both snowflakes of Bethlehem,
in His palms, for His arrangement—

No two miracles,
ever alike.

Snowflakes of Bethlehem, II

Both snowflakes of Bethlehem
fall on blessed manger,
drift into spirit,
upon birth hands of Christ.

One palm, Our Redeemer
Other palm, World Healer—
no two miracles—ever
quite alike.

Capricorn

I, too, was born in the tattered age of the snow goat,
the age of the capriole,
God's leap for humanity,
the hollowed-horn of music,
from angels anchored on the Old Mountain.
So, I leave the sea, speak only to Saturn—
who offers me a landscape
of such prudent peaks. I climb
to eventual demise, say around Augustus' tax time.
Caesar charges me *land;*
leaves me nothing but *scape*.
Over the Old Mountain,
I am ridiculed in the wake of the ringed star
darkening to the one, brightly shone,
over Bethlehem. Skidproof, I am certain
to see a full woman with a scant man.
The goatskins of the drummer
summon the majestic at hand.
Capricious, I flee
from the Nativity scene, on a cloud boat.
And leave, the boy Jesus,
to be the world's scapegoat.

The SecrIt of Christmas

It stays the same.

It is in my hometown.

It can't be far away.

It came upon…

Its time is here.

It is, baby, please come home.

It is the only time *merry* and *little* go so well together.

It is thought of any bird in any fruited tree.

It is the drum in the desert.

It is the true Thanksgiving.

Its season begins with birth of Him, reason for sky, sand, sea.

It is NativITy.

As on a Wintry Plain

The old ghosts won't haunt, still you lift a ride,
take a team of eight by gossamer reins,
colorless journey, save the chestnut sleigh,
through barest of birches, no limbs to hide,
except your sparse bones in their waning lives,
to scarve you or scar you, whatever pain
that will encourage the ghosts, *mush* again,
their eyes of white wolves running in full stride.

What keeps you, child, on such long, wintry plain—
the blush ahead is not one of summer;
it is last regret, a light in the fog,
to give you false wish, a fool's wonder.
The ghosts break for last bits of prairie grain,
then abandon lift to the face of God.

Voyeur to the World

Mary had enough linen
to erect an immaculate curtain
before the makeshift manger.

Wasn't his birth a private matter?
Wasn't it a private winter?

Even the bluest lights over Bethlehem
telescoped in for a piece of the act.

What would you do—
with oxen, donkeys,
inspecting chickens—
brooding around you?

The novice drummer banging his pipes,
a few spooked shepherds—
ruffled angel banging her pipes—

What would you do—
Build a do-not-disturb petting zoo?

No. You do nothing.

It was Mary who showed
the wondering world—
silence works.

It was Mary who opened
the heart of Israel, all timeless borders,
as if to say,

Enter. Love him.
But I have loved him first.

Tree Topper

I
am
the
love
above,
Gloria
present,
watchful,
spreading
jubilation,
I, identified
Angel, the Lord

The Marriage of Snow

Somewhere, the hero for whom you've waited
comes to you through the parting snow,
offers a kind hand that recently won
an old war. You have imagined this
tableau in your mind, a thousand ceremonies,
and now it is new. The trees are veiled,
prepared to limb the bouquet. You have
seen yourself through a most patient
engagement. Then, birds beading
south suddenly turn and lift your train
into the ring-bear air. Even the sky,
in its omniscient indifference,
says, *Yes*. Come to him, then,
during this marriage of snow.
Tender your borrowed dream
among the fields of blue gathers. No
time of year, nothing, can keep a promise
like the dearth and death of December.
If love can reach you through
this most impassable storm, with
nothing but a dying branch to sign
as your witness, then love
has seen you, old,
with your whitest of hair down,
blue, with the dampest of unseasonable smiles,
borrowed, unwilling to grace
the new day.
Yes, love has seen you through this;
and, pardon the cliché',
is here to stay.

I Am a Poor Boy, Too

There is a boy in the desert	*Reach me*
Keeping time on animal skins	*Ah, for music they die*
He is wise among kings and their riches	*Teach me*
He worships a babe in the barn	*Or is the counselor I*
His coat is sparse, but of many blunders	*My rhythms*
Poverty, neglect, wounds	*Silent dusk's only tune*
He is night wind and little lamb	*Please, boy;*
Lowly eye of the sky	*Touch my lain full moon*
There is a boy in the desert	*There is a call for you, too*
Kicked among gold and myrrh	*Count on me, calmly*
And when, at last, he turns from the manger	*With my one need*
It is he who inherits the earth	*Beat me*

Mary Magdalene: An Equal-Rights Amendment

If she were a prostitute, where are the stories of Roman sires
and silver acquisitions up Her sleeve—the purloined fruits of
Her mercenary enticements, obvious analogies to Eve? *The Bible*
weds Her name with love; we, ash of the artifact, assume
it's for sex—She-Shame of the Scriptures, Sister Sodom spreading
Gomorrah's venereal hex.

Her dance card would have been proverbially full
at the Last Supper among mortal grins and dorsal knives.
Why not the invite for Magdalene, the Lenten Lolita?
Well, perhaps HIStory crucifies her a concubine, worships Her
a whore, denies the title *disciple* –She the First Apostle
of the Table in form of chair and board.

And didn't She do what twelve chosen could not—
lay her desire down for our lives—give its object—the Son of Man—
back to God? She'd be the first to admit the Lord's Angel, uplift
of wings, beat her there to the Stone of Perpetual Morning—
her hands, fresh spices rising to the air. And who ever approached
more closely than She to being His wife, bedding holy flesh,
moving forward with the next Joyous Child?

Our Savior bestowed Simon *The Rock,* John and James
Sons of Thunder. Let legend list Judas *Iskariot* the *iota risk*—
and Mary Magdalene, *First Lady Forever, Woman of Wonder.*
He selected this Swan to walk at His right hand.
Is that not symbol enough? If not, imagine a dozen for dinner
aligned behind Him like ganders fraying over the goose's crumbs.

Twin millennia ago, a great man crossed over;
a lady of licentious rumor lost Her pure lover. Immaculate Procreation
placed on Eternal Hold. It was this—the High Hush—for a score
of centuries that Christian myth, not Magdalene, peddled and sold.
Isn't time we resurrected the greatest story never told?

Acolytes

As shepherds approached the manger,
canes a-light with faith abound,
those bowed turned
to witness the procession, litany in the desert,
of pastoral vestments, staffs, and gowns.

Sweet Mary held earth's Candle,
and, for a moment, all at kneel stood.
Star of Bethlehem, merely, wick and flicker
to the Nova newborn who was to bring the world
peace and a will of good.

When we are, first, children of our churches,
like the shepherds, we walk to bring the Candle, light,
down the sanctuary to the altar—
to assist is the gift of acolytes.

Mesopotamia

Here is my camel, Mesopotamia,
humpsteed of peace, rustled by two-fisted wrists:
a gush of Arab seize and clutch-cross of Christianity.

After lapse of lost centuries,
her first straw returns to me.

Come, Mesopotamia,
color of dune.
Lead me to the purge,
this remarriage of waters—
Tigris, Euphrates.
Lead me to drink, desert horse,
beneath one true moon.

Mesopotamia, renamed, restored
mounted to redress—
a teethe, a team of beasts bow
at your mouth, at last, without harness.

Gone are the dromedreary,
cacophony of *Iraq*.
Blessing rides high,
prepared for attack.

To the cradle-altar, Mesopotamia,
for a birth, a wedding without
political swords, torn garments, despotic religion—
ceremony serene—oasis forgiven.

Guide, Mesopotamia,
lift the hearse from your face.
Nod to the nuptial party in place,
the dark tails of honor, white sands of grace.

The Bell of Great Paul

Great Paul is the largest bell in the United Kingdom;
it is located at St. Paul's Cathedral, London.

My mother never knew London, no jeweled heir.
Big Ben clocked for other tourists; The Queen, no time to spare.
Still, the guard changed when she lost my father.
The only crown she obeyed bowed breathlessly to her feet.

She never dreamed he'd leave upon the wake of winter.
She, who tended his cracked lungs through the tolling fall.
But these past Christmas Days, since her soldier passed away,
She hears the Bell of Great Paul.

The Feast of Stephen, each New Year,
Its frost-born casting swings for her swoon.
No harmony, no measure, off pitch,
A treasure out of tune.

As she walks the snow sweeps of Rose Hill Cemetery,
The peal sweeps her from earthly despair.

Father, we never thought you'd die upon the first chimes of winter.
The clime's air roped us coldly without your commanding call.
Now, the home tins are caroling, every time you ring
The faithful Bell of Great Paul.

My soul was a Gothic tower,
Looking out, lifelong, for approval's ding to pull me through.
My walls grew harsher with the dong-reject of every hour.
My deaf tongue removed itself and disrespected you.

Dad, it took a burned palm to show us how to love you.
Beneath your star, we swept an empty manger stall.
But on this Christmas Eve, as your spirit moves her sleeve,
Mom feels the love that moves us all.

We hear the Bell of Great Paul.

--for C. Paul Thompson

Mauve and Amethyst

Purple the sky,
Purple His lips,
Purple Christ's heart,
Purple the waves that bore three ships,
Purple the brood of beasts, their evince of mist,
Purple the partridge first morning,
Purple the one kiss,

So why aren't the dyes of Christmas
Mauve and Amethyst?

The Snow Geese

the snow geese
precipitate the sky

with winter
wings

V-trekked
beak direct
any route, but circumspect

a rage of horns resounding
across the one true open road

flurrious flock
insistent that fall yield
the right of way

their down drifts
across the dark lake
of frosted reeds,
& the last departing loon

autumn abandoned
the gaggle rules,
accumulates in a solstice sky—
their cornet's cry
announces in stentorian tune

He He
as as
we

comes again
& soon

On Unseasonably

A Polite Rain

Permission to pour?
inquires the sky at breakfast,
its kettle of condensation
unable to keep
the morning brew back.

Why, of course!
my dry retort.

For when my brick throat
& slick coat are thirsty,
I like my clouds like my coffee—

thicker, billowing, & black.

--for JW

The Snow Globe

He steps outside and looks at a house of fit-glass
Upstairs, Mom and Dad create a white-fit fury
He tells his sorrow, *In time, lad, this, too, shall pass*
In his hand, invisible hatchet to bury

It's his house, too; he could enter without a knock
Take his rightful place beneath warped blue ceiling
Suspend himself in anger—whatever will shock
His folks to break their freeze and to kindle healing

Instead, the boy places his palm on the window
And breathes an imprint to cold-steam his despair
A wave farewell, a wispy feather to undo
Firm ground of two villagers in their selfish air

Through stop-stern water—parents dare him to make them
The boy could use a good laugh, and so he shakes them

Unseasonably Lumped

Look low,
my oldest sister, Susan, directed
from the garland stair.
Has Santa even been here?
Nod, John, if you see anything bright and shiny.
Did Santa forget to festoon our home?
Let's tiptoe down, now!
Someone go and stir Mom and Dad around.

All that Santa left was a scarlet stain.
The plush 70s shag carpet, an empty evergreen plain.

Look, she shifted into philosophical verse, *it could be worse,*
as her voice drove the holiday hearse.
Let's wait, let's wait, to hear what the folks explain first.

There were no gifts we kids were to be receiving—
Santa's sleigh, a distant bell shake on the sterile horizon.
Christmas was only coming through in carols of pain.
Needle-teeth on the tinsel spoke,
but I could read neither boughs nor braces.

Christmas 1972, I was a boy of nine, still, still, still—
a true believer.
Then stone-coal disappointment locked my mother
on Medusa's mattress inside a shale bedroom.
It was some financial deal my Dad had the gall
to do behind her back, announced to all at church,
then fade to black.
Home, she scurried, like the mouse she was
in his trap   to sorrow's shack.

And, we minors, we had become…unseasonably lumped.

Ok, Susan spoke to the wall grinning with greeting cards.
I'll start to fix something quick—
pudding or corn casserole, I don't recall—
What mattered, the girl was in the kitchen—apron, ache, and all,
though her consolation cooking made me sick.

Unseasonably Lumped

On Unseasonably

Unseasonably Lumped

On our treetop, depending on the angle,
an angel turned into a crystal cross.
When the eve of dysfunction descended,
Susan turned into the pistol-boss.
Bless her range. Bless her cross.
Bang! Bang! He's dead, John.
That is how I learned…there was no Santa Claus.

That year, there were no gifts we kids were to be receiving—
Santa's sleigh, a distant bell shake on the sterile horizon.
That year, the Hollies sung of a long woman in black dress,
wrapped around my mother's countenance, no less.
And I've grown to betray her beauty by what I confess.

I spoke, *Yuletide, you're over.*
That's all Santa's list wrote.
Put down the cherry brandy.
Grab your coat.
The season stuck like pecan brittle in my third-grade throat.

I'll make it up to you, son, when you're ten.

I never loved or hated her more than then.

At Christmas, indeed, in bleed,
the child is coddler to the man.

Cornucopia / Corn of Coping You

The living fruit
still on the vine,
bold in branches,
gather around
my father's November coffin
to offer conversation—
who is to partake
in his acres and debt?
Daddy is a licked cone
on the table of abundant death.
His corpse is driving
one more load
of produce home;
and the living fruit worships and wets.

My mother sits
in the front of the sanctuary, widow
weaving a hymnal
through her free hands.
The organist pipes
grace and grain
from the usual tubes.
Mom's own foot plays taps
to the inaugural
notes of the prelude.
The corn of fifty-odd years
on her small toe
softens, disappears
by verse two.

Resolutions

The child resolves to pick up bounced balls
if Dad will curtail his drinking.

Mom rakes her mind and porch, self-absorbed,
Leaves are for leaving, she's been thinking.

For old time's sake, the house tends these aches
And prepares for empty, dysfunctional weather.

A bottle cached upstairs, toy soldiers enlisted, everywhere,
a woman pulling her life and gift-luggage together—

Sleighn (Pain's Quatrain)

The wounded, dear, leap the highest.

Blue-funk's fog beams a bloody nose.

The soul drips deep sighs of crimson.

Those aren't roses lain in the snow.

Christmas After Dad Passed

Do not misinterpret the gesture, love.

I do not wish you dead;

But here are box directions for the gift rifle

Complete with free map to the shed.

Down County

It is Christmas Eve; and, down county,
tribal white men are putting on white.
They summon the horses out of the barn.
The wind alone causes their fetlocks to fright.

Tribal white men are putting on white.
I see them in the far pasture, grazing a most deadly gift.
The wind alone causes their locks to ignite.
My mom bars the door, her arms like a cross.

I see men in the star pasture, grazing for deadly-kiss gift.
Upon fast horses, they circle like a mistletoe wreath.
My mom bars the door, her arms like a cross.
The gift of fire emerges between a ribbon of sheets.

Upon fast horses, the men circle like a holiday wreath.
As prejudiced heads turn toward the house where all is coal.
The gift of fire emerges between a ribbon of sheets.
It is late in the evening; neither my father nor brother are home.

As prejudiced heads turn toward the coal house,
the cross that is my mother's arms gives way to leg shakes.
It is late evening; neither my father nor brother are home.
The snow on the porch gives a moan, or is it an ache?

The cross that is my mother's arms gives way to the shakes.
White men in an enamel cloud cause decay to make a char-white place.
Snow on our porch gives a moan, or is it an ache?
Coal mom and coal daddy offer their gifts to the Christian right.

White men in an enamel cloud cause decay to make a white palace.
We dream for a White Christmas, after all, downy country—
Once soul mom and soul daddy offer their gifts
And scream for their babes to stride out of the barn.

Your Frozen Body Is a Winter Wonderland

If I wish you anything,
you racist extremity,
I wish you death by frostbite.

Ironic as iced heat, isn't it?
To find yourself—alone—
blizzard for one—
Noel nowhere—
hours past chilblain,
trench foot—your cells
forming glace
stalagmites, stalactites
that you cannot see,
but only feel—
suddenly, you can't even do that—
as they and the outermost limbs of your skin
darken, blacken, *niggrify*
to a cold, toxic halt.

Your blue body catches up
with this more preferable hue.

The next morning
a whites-only search party,
comprised of your hot-toddy buddies,
unwraps a patch of enlightened snow,
to find the first Christmas corpse.

And on this day, as a boy,
you received some ranger of rescue
mounted on a glacier getaway horse.

Christmas Rodeo

The angels weren't angels,
but quiescent queens of the rodeo.

The beasts were one composite bull—
only the desert spur wanted to ride.

Jesus was roped into being
the clown and star of the dirt studio.

And Joseph had knowledge of Mary,
but he couldn't stay on for 8 seconds.

Ladies and gents,
stand a few feet back
from the fence of redemption, repentance
that rises in the most extreme degrees, like a long sentence
in the dusts of December,
the chutes of July.

December Dismissal

The schoolmarm dismisses
her coven of kids
to brew in the toils
and troubles of mid-December.

Each trick,
in his or her own breaking way,
whisks or sashays
down the paper-flaked corridor.

Each,
save one,
wishes 'marm
a perfunctory *Merry Christmas*.

The old, perturbed teach
hinges on the glare of omission
like a door-slammed witch,
whose temper like the days are shorter.

She grimaces in silent-ignite return—
that, until January 2nd, will burn—

An apology is in order!

--for Mary Stout

Love and Logic

If I rescue the children's argument,
it will explode
like a gas pump selling fire.

I look into fighting eyes—
as if to drift—
I know, I know.

The room cools.

I take a broom
and whisk
the white ash of anger.

How lovely the silence
settled in this snow.

Pageant

And it came to pass,
That in those days and in these days,
That nothing rhymes with *pageant.*
Shepherds in their sheets from home
Scratch their urgent heads. Nothing.
The ox and lamb tangent
attempt to rhyme. Nothing for this pageant.
An agent from the Lord regrets
Nothing in the angel's flagellant wings
Flings a rhyme with *pageant.*
The baby-boy doll, fresh purchase from the mall,
Wrapped in bluest blanket
Flips over in frustration
Like a page, the gent
Cannot Christmas-morn a miracle
Lyric to rhyme with *pageant.*

Paper Rudolph

The same *r* that serves first letter to *Rudolph,*
and *red-nosed* and *reindeer*—is the same *r*
in *runaway.*

And, girl, your laptop mouse
is a creature stirring
for a getaway sleigh.

Who are you chatting with tonight?
The regular Rex, who, if you meet him—
promises to pay?

Hovering over your dreamscape screen,
a decorative Rudolph
of papier-mache.

He, too, began life torn in strips,
like your innocence—
when you were eight.

Six winters back,
a secret Santa slipped you a stocking
and unwrapped a world of giving pain.

You could just beat yourself like a piñata,
or, better, that paper Rudolph, who witnessed all,
but wouldn't antler-utter a damn thing.

Shopping at home,
at last, you're in charge of stage and tone—
or is this all a reindeer game?

Neigh Day

Something's disturbed
in the stable.

Three hands and a first-year
who refuses her hay.

No oxen or sheep just backwoods asses,
so there goes pleasant fable.

A virgin at the sable light of conception,
the palms at her wrists and feet, not there to pray.

Above her, any Joe, a foreman, Star of Danger,
bearing forearms resolved and able—

And Bethlehem
mangers away.

Bluestockings

After Dorothy Parker

Along the west end
of blazed fireplace,
the J's hang in row—
one for sorrow,
idleness, friend, and foe.
Blush above embers,
noosed feet and soles,
three bags for candy,
one dump for coal.
My family roasts here,
one can only hope
that Santa Claus
christens the evening
with one perfect rope.

The Moon at Christmas

Silver and gold, silver and gold,
She hangs her own tinsel, constant and cold.
A glint of frost mint in the yuletide sky—
Sleep well, little children. She serves as first spy
for the coming of Claus and eight in front of the sleigh.
The moon marks the shine on the milk-and-goodie plate.
A night for the silent, with no beast to fear,
in absence, the moon is ambassador for the midnight clear.

Upon the house tops, fir boughs, and dreams,
the moon licks the blades skating over streams.
Swaddled in a sigh, a world of peace to uncover,
the moon never forgets: her purpose for lovers.
She knows them by heart—come, faithful, to face her.
She, who shone first light, on a face in the manger.

The Ocean at Christmas

I have never seen three mermaids wreathed in mistletoe.
Nor heard the anchors of Christmas chiming underwater.
Nautical or nice, does the ocean know it's Christmastime?
From sand to snow—Christ, does Santa even seaside bother?

Now, I've eaten my spoon of oyster stew
And a few other sea-blime, seasonal dishes;
but I gainsay you'll ever see a ship as saltwater sleigh,
Wishing you a Merry Fishmas.

A red sail teamed with an evergreen tossed at sea
Will not undo the waves of perpetual blue.
It's clear as midnight upon me, my bleak matey,
This terrestrial festival wants pittance to do with you.

Glutton for Christmas Punishment

You cool on a cushion-plate
burning for the glass at your side—
a manger of milk
decked in crystal and white.
The coming of Claus is a chance
FAT as a fed elf.
You've a list filled with plum-wishes
for redeeming yourself.

These should be enough—your treats on a tray
to effect reindeer on the roof—and Savior and sleigh.
But, it sifts through you like sugar, cookie,
first-hand sight of your folks, kneeled, with second-hand goods,
backlit by a marathon holiday movie upon midnight tube.
Christmas comes wrapped with the usual wounds.

All Abhorred—*The Polar Express*—The Movie

A Movie Review

As adults, we kept the anticipation to ourselves—
the long-awaited release of the year's
blockbuster-animated feature—
be it by Dreamworks, Disney, or Pixar.

In November 2004, the re-election of Bush
was a snooze. What Americans, young and old alike,
were truly rooting for was the toot-toot
of the *The Polar Express* in the theaters—opening
Wednesday, November 10th.
We took sick days, personal days, bereavement days,
fake doctor appointments to grab some cash,
a cab and head for a day at the matinee.

There, two-feet above the rest of the juvenile crowd,
we realized it—a fact as hard as no Santa Claus:
Something, indeed, was lost in translation—
from storybook to screen.

The Polar Express had skidded off
the slippery reel of film and landed a movie-house flop.

Sigh. The big kids in the dark that day
had been children when the Caldecott-winning book
was first shelved in 1985. It took our entire
transformation into grown-ups to witness
the boy, the bell, the journey to the elves
come to life. Warm buttered popcorn couldn't soothe us.

That night, the reviews, theories poured over
the media like a large soda filling a small cup.
Simply put, you can't stretch a children's story
into a full-length feature film without assuming
liberties that damage the initial charm of
the book and illustrations. That was the nice review.

All Aborred—

All Abhorred—

Here are the naughty ones…
What was Castle Rock, home to Stephen King's maniacal miracles,
doing as chief producer to the film? Each village looked
like it was waiting for the next serial killer to nab
fresh kids/slash/victims on the shanty porches.
Santa looked like Cujo in red-and-white drag.
And the elves up north weren't on Santa's list;
they looked like mug shots on the sex-offender list.

And what was Tom Hanks thinking
while playing/voicing five parts.
Joanne Woodward took on less in *The Three Faces of Eve.*
The Hero Boy Narrator, The Boy's Father,
The Conductor, Hobo, and Santa—
Frankly, doesn't Hanks realize
that other actors need work, too—
not a very charitable act to do—
not quite Christmassy.

Blunders, bloopers, and ballyhoo are passengers, too.
In fact, they avalanche—
minors risking their lives traipsing across boxcars
in pursuit of a runaway ticket—that—*hello*—
is sticking in a vent—
the coupling of hot chocolate with dancing porters—
(Kids, please, do not try this at home)—
a musical number, by the way, that Broadway
would've darkened before the first marshmallow plopped.

And the music—the music did more for earmuff sales
that winter than Boss Blizzard!

Yes, we detested it, loathed the life out of it.
We wanted our money back, but what was the use?
Not even the Oscars nominated this wrecked caboose—
in an Animated Category most thought
the film couldn't lose.
The Polar Express movie was the first gift refused.

We walked out of the theatres down disappointed snow tracks.
Wait-'til-next-year, a distant engine steamed,
when *The Polar Express returns a hit on IMAX!*

Sissy Spacek

Born on December 25, 1949

Born Mary—
Texas, too, has its one star,
shining over birth home or hospital
this Christmas Day
before the cold of the Cold War.
And three wise men are there
direct from the West—
a producer, a director, an agent.
But it is the baby girl who bears the gifts—
beautiful simplicity,
acting range wider than the Panhandle.

She will cause audiences to struggle
between mercy and horror
in the name and flames of Carrie White.
It is she who will bring dignity
to county music, to thousands
who thought they were beneath it.
Her Beth will search the scours of South America,
expose our own government to bring Charles home.

Ok, one character will sleep with Mel Gibson
as good cinematography holds back a river.
And her Babe Magrath will rope us all
when she accessorizes her desperate neck
with a chandelier.

Before Halle Berry makes film history,
Ruth Fowler's conspiring grief in the bedroom
will give her a monster run for Hollywood's top prize.

Texas knew, it just knew, in the dust of December—
the longhorn could tell by the lone star
in baby's eyes.

American Traffic

Phillip Nicholas Swimm hadn't biked since he was a boy.
Now, his buttocks were battling to prevent a seat,
whose surface area, like the Grinch's heart,
was two sizes too small, from disappearing indefinitely
up his private chimney flue. Phil Swimm
was aboard the hybrid Schwinn
he bought last Christmas
to prove a point to a gullible America.

There he rides, along RAGBRAI,
the Des Moines *Register's* Annual Great Bike Race
Across Iowa, a needle of sorts in a very fit haystack,
with his group of cyclists the PEDAL PHILS.
The team's name is garnering attention,
though Phillip wishes to remain incognito.

What turned him against Homeland Security
is really anyone's guess. Perhaps he has no real beef,
but just longs for some press. For that evening,
while the rest of the RAGBRAIers are sleeping,
our man Swimm, a stealthy Santa, plans to steal
anyone's car, anyone in Eldon, Iowa, off Highway 30,
and smash into the American Gothic house,
destroying, at least damaging, all that is good,
decent, and reliable on our porches and lawns.
That certainly won't effect a smile from Grant Wood's
sister, his dentist, or anyone drawing a salary
in the name of security across the United States soon.

Then, Phil will steal away back to his tent,
perch on his bike the next morn, a most innocent bird.
The radios about will buzz and flitter, *Everyone heard?*
Was it some kid on a joyride or Islam on a mission?
And still they ride, RAGBRAIers, with FBI saddled
to both sides. Phil breaks for no one; not a bureaucrat
will ask him.

The sky transcends from code orange to nose red.
When the fog of the feds ends,
Phillip Swimm travels forth, like Rudolph, to the head.

Copyright Santa Claus

Trademark laws, a restrictive clause,
reined a writer form penning about
a certain beverage-with-leverage Santa Claus.

Rude-awful.

The scribe floats in a fog.

On Fizzer, On Capper,
On Killjoyer,   On Pause—

A journalist can banter about any Santa;
but a poet, no such cause.

Why papers sell more pages
than poetry's few rooms.

Free speech, impeached,
stuffed in a stocking filled of flaws.

A Mist Christmas

Good writer that she is,
Marian, quick-witted in her kitchen,
Creates an anagram
Out of the word *Christmas:*

MIST CHARS.

She understands Mist—
As in Mist, Oregon,
Her beloved hometown
Where the meadowlark
Sweeps over a breath of Oregon grape flower,
As the towering Douglas fir
Watches from a lookout
Over the winding Columbia River
Filled with square-dancing beavers
And all that state-symbol stuff.

But nothing of charring reminds her of Mist.
Meanwhile, the holiday duck in her oven
Singes to a crisp.

--for Marian Clark

The Cedar Waxwing

The cedar waxwing is one of the few animals that faces sickness or death due to intoxication from eating fermented fruit, usually whole.

The cedar waxwing,
poor intoxicated thing,
tips atop a wintry fence, wired.
Drunk from fermented punch
it swooped for lunch
and swallowed
the bowl of citrus contents, entire.

Come, chickadee, with hot coffee.
Enter, cardinal, with cloth of remedy cubes.
Assist, partridge, with two aspirin.
Be mindful, all three, of wing's spin and drool.

Oh, cedar waxwing, December's
sloshed and smashed darling,
is it reasonable to tag you,
the holiday *buzzard*.

Thank goodness that tree
doesn't nest the season's office party,
or my, pie-eyed pickle,
you'd be fired.

Persephone on Holiday

Like Christ, she, too ascends
with deliverance of spring;
but the lavender storms near Easter
steal her thunder.

Her hopeful bones remove Hell,
itself a mammoth stone.
She walks this dirt and hangs herself
like fresh linen before a sanctuary transfixed
on Him, another tombed wonder.

Oh, she brings the green,
largely unseen;
the gratitude received lost
in a March-gone-Madness world.

In her cool, honey hair,
the girl presses every lily on earth,
in blithe despair,
every lily, every lily,
each petal of pearl.

Bethlehem, Pennsylvania

First and forever born—
A night, a year, an age.
Mother is on maternal leave 'til spring.
Father is a new-hire wage.

And there, child, you lie, transfixed,
In Mid-Atlantic manger down.
To the up-East, a star lights off Broadway.
To the west, the haunts of Allentown.

Absent beasts quicken to warmer prairie.
Angel of Mercy booked in Hollywood.
Gathered around you, kid, hand-me-down Lionel trains,
And your first pair of crocheted workman's boots.

Yes, Aunt Philadelphia is at her Christmas knitting.
She stews upon a skittish stool.
In this evening of hurt—Behold, a shirt—
She twists the collar blue.

Outside, the factories are stacked against you, child,
Like the odds of getting good meat on next noon's plate.
Nightshift snow angels make blades of steel.
Flakes of smoke fall on their haloes of keystone gray.

Three drug dealers have walked the urban desert
To crack the addict's call.
Pop Joe needs a hit of amyl anything.
Ma Mary, a retro-dose of Demarol.

Such steel-clad clarity, narcotic nativity,
Strung out like Auntie's yarn.
Another boy born in discounted basement,
Another baby in the barn.

A Retrospective

Opening the wraps of unwanteds
under the fir tent
after a wishful nap,
you retrace your steps—
out the walk,
to the mall,
that's it—
you're back on
Santa's lap—appalled—
this is your chance, kid,
go ahead and ask:
Just what in the world
am I supposed to do with that?
Before his belly can answer,
undaunted, give his chin a slap.

The Mother of Trees

God refused to fit her in evergreen fir,
so she slips on the ice of winter kills—
haggard branches, egg empty,
hard-candy, gossamer-gloved,
nesting nothing but wicked debris.

Bereaved, her hanging glass
crosses the wires, detours the streets.
Chaos and crystal, in freeze-frame,
she leans.

Her children, long left her,
seeking fleeting careers in bags of leaves.
Her husband, faithless as summer;
none, but hard wind, to solicit as lover.

Snowblind from spring,
the mother of trees
heavies as she blows,
bereft in clinging beauty,
foreboding pose.

She crackles like a hidden witch,
bends her broom over the pitch roof,

and breaks the stone house

where a once beloved family

once trusted her roots.

Winter Caves

These were the first fires, first sparks
to trigger living-room trees.
The inaugural blanket spread leather here
to cover eons of freeze.
The mother of Mary's mother
drew a vision on smoke-wreathed wall.
Her daughter's daughter to bear
the bones of a baby to frame one and all.

The first gifts were patience and silence
bound by hunter's unknowing scars,
gathered in round garland of raw humanity,
spoken as an omen of eternal star.
The barbaric, the undocumented, the unheard of—
encrusted together to clear hearts for coming love.

Ultimate Solstice

Winter is timeless to me now;
no hourglass can contain it.
The shape of *8* has shattered;
snow shakes, loose and free.
The grain that was April
lies still like a lost amusement
beneath a bed of infinite ice.
The hills are white wrinkles
where children mockingly sleigh.
I take a tip of one blade
to pick at my face.
I would tell them—
as I tell myself—
to ease in from the cold;
but winter is timeless—
less these ticks of age.
Anyone caught counting—
drifts in vain

All About Christmas Eve

I met my charm-school rival, Margo,
At the Stage Door General Store.
The snow was auditioning Christmas Eve.
Harried, I nipped-and-tucked away from her
Behind the Pringles and Ruffles chips,
Then I touched a ruffle on the bitch's printed sleeve.

Miss Channing didn't recognize
My Sarah Siddons Award-winning face at first,
Then her publicity teeth threw open the sash wide.
In a pirouette tete-a-tete, we stunningly delivered
The lines both had long rehearsed,
Secretly conceding both the fire and music had died.

In a kiss between boozy, fabulous freaks,
We missed, by considerable inches, each other's rouged cheeks.
Then we wormed our way to the front of the line.
I, Eve, the ingénue,
Acquired a trench-coat penchant for Mountain Dew martinis;
Margo, for salted peanuts, and old-bird wine.

We stepped outside into wassail-waiting taxi cab.
Her sharp tongue corked open a 750 ml glass.
Precipitation on the roof beat like footsteps on the ceiling—
Or was God providing—
There on the corner of Addison & DeWitt—
Holiday knives to stab in each other's backs?

She raised a bottle to Broadway.
I lifted a refundable to applause.
I admitted to sleeping
With every writer and director with a contract offer.
Margo replied,
Hell, Eve, in an hour I'm in bed with Santa Claus.

The Dew was drunk, and the wine at home.
Coldly, I made my usual, pronounced, elegant turn.
I would have offered my heart for trophy warmth, just then,
But neither of us had a heart to burn.
Margo took her seat belt and buckled her pride in tight,
And spoke, *To all a Merry Christmas, and to Eve, a bumpy life.*

The Mrs.

Mrs. Claus is a chain smoker,
Puffing SOS goodies
From the Arctic to the waiting world.
Tired of delicates freezing on the line,
Mrs. Claus was first to bake her bra
In an effort to liberate iced underwear.
Oh, yes, she oversees the elves;
But it is Santa whom she nicks
little man.
Can you guess willy-why?
I bet you candy-cane can!

Anna Anaesthesia

Anna sat on Santa's lap
and spoke in North Pole dialect,
All I want for Christmas is a syringe.

Kris Kringle cringed.

He waved his sausage fingers
in a *Ho, ho, no, Anna—the drugs will kill you.*
Is there something else, kitten, the cat can give you?

Then, Anna plunged into her knitted sleeve,
barreled up an arm of garment
to reveal a team of eight perfect pricks—
prancing the sky that was her skin.
Her addiction told, for overnight overdose,
she needed a ninth hole—
one familiar with blue-fog and a tiny red nose.

Under the pine, under her tree—

Anna was looking for a another kind of needle
to stick and chase away the peppermint pain,
strapping a rubber stocking

on bicep,
            on tricep,
pulling it tightly to expose the last virgin vein,

looking for a hark-the-heroin angel high,
to thumb a chloroform ride on Old Claus' sleigh—
a festive fix, lying betwixt gifts of dolls and trains.

What she was running from was
what she had become—

pulling it tightly, dear, like a rein.

St. Nick's Limerick

Who's that shaking my shingle?
Causing tinsel to tingle?
Better be insured—
Pass the reindeer word—
Your sleigh's appraised, Kris Kringle.

Dasher

Those Aerial
Antlers Are
Not Deer,
You See,

PLACE

The Sleigh
Is Pulled
Each Year
By Caribou—

SANTA

And You
Are No
Longer Dear
To Me—
CLAUS

Who Can
Pull The
Reins In
On You?
HERE

IV
On Epiphany

Prologue

this is time travel
of ancient ways,
discipled nights,
twelve-star gaze,
the desert step,
walk of three winds,
their prayer, fourth air,
sung breath of hymn;
be there beasts, be they wise,
beneath light of fruited sky;
this Eden after Eve;
He is wrapped and present—believe, believe

NOTE: The number of words in each
of the following month passages
equals the number of days
in that month.

January

First Day of Epiphany

A star rings in the east,
brightest toast, confetti sky.
Diapered in snow, Earth a newborn,
balloon-blue.
We three go forth.
Gaspar,
Melchior,
Balthazaar pray…
He isn't king
for a day.

February

Second Day of Epiphany

Like a mother in the womb of memory—
herself being born—
we hear a heartbeat.
It rejects the arrow, dismisses myth,
saved by seal of sweet Mary's kiss.

March

Third Day of Epiphany

The wind a lamb's shake
begins our charmed day.
Shepherds greet us,
descendants of Abraham's ken.
The meekest approaches, prophecizes:
Christ is the lamb who will be shepherd to all men.

April

Fourth Day Epiphany

An angel appears,
offers a lily,
places petal on palm.
The sky becomes a dark rose.
We wise are fools, Magi silly.
Tombs taunt princely feet.
Rise, thorn and stone.

May

Fifth Day of Epiphany

Iris hour, open-hand flower,
permits, allows.
We basket earth's gifts—
gold, myrrh, frankincense.
We priests, we astronomers, we believe.
We'll see our king—
as the fruitless Negev
bears faith in Spring.

June

Sixth Day of Epiphany

Lady Inquisition summers on evanescent wings—
bugs, stings.
Were we at the manger first night?
Did twelve moons morn?
Perhaps a year hatched—
To Jospeh's garden-home to jar Herod's swarm!

July

Seventh Day of Epiphany

No fires work the east/
No firmament-fuse cracks the west.
All Israel stilled—
the world, willing, dowses its breath.
Our humbled triumvirate resting, Lord, too—
in honor
in image of You.

August

Eighth Day of Epiphany

We come to Dead Sea,
denied rebirth, drink.
Desiccant stars long, thirst.
A dromedary sips, throat to salt, dirt.
Heat hushes voice-air.
Low body, water, on its knees
in perpetual prayer.

September

Ninth Day of Epiphany

We, too, pupils schooled—
sky, sapphire board—
Star of Bethlehem, master, ruler.
Reckoned by discipline,
we pass infinity,
Earth's shortest breath test.
Question in the east,
Answer in the west.

October

Tenth Day of Epiphany

Somewhere, someone inters Immaculate Seed—
It is behind us now;
It is irreversible future.
Gabriel's year to harvest,
glebes of shepherds.
When were we not ripe, God?
Blessed for your picking?

November

Eleventh Day of Epiphany

Famined, faint,
we know not pilgrimage's end.
Dry-mouthed,
we taste the Old Testament,
seasoned exodus.
We step, still, in wonder
on giving leaves.
Lord, we are portions feasting for thee.

December

Twelfth Day of Epiphany

To believe in us now is to tempt theory.
Fit for nativity—
matters us not.
Christ born, here—
Savior, Redeemer.
We, His Servants.
We are not gifted.
We are in love.